THE TEACHINGS OF
SHRI KRISHNA

THE TEACHINGS OF SHRI KRISHNA

A Guide to Overcoming Life's Challenges through Shri Krishna's Teachings

Wisdom for Modern Times

THE ORIGINAL LEGENDARY WORK BY: -
SACHIN PRAJAPATI

While every precaution has been taken in preparing this book, the publisher assumes no responsibility for errors or omissions, or for damages resulting from using the information contained herein.
THE TEACHINGS OF SHRI KRISHNA
First edition. March 10, 2024.
Copyright © 2024 Sachin Prajapati.
Written by Sachin Prajapati.

Dedicated

To The Readers of The Book

Table of Content

INTRODUCTION

Who is Shri Krishna?

Lord Shri Krishna is the Supreme Personality. He is one of Hinduism's most renowned deities and is believed to be Lord Vishnu's eighth avatar (incarnation). He is acknowledged not only in Hinduism but also in Jainism and Buddhism, where he is known as Vasudeva and Kanha, respectively.

Lord Shri Krishna is well-known for his intellect, valor, and teachings on karma and dharma. He is regarded as a great warrior, diplomat, ideal friend, legendary teacher, advisor, outstanding leader, ocean of knowledge, motivator, bright student, Master of Communication, and excellent philosopher.

Shri Krishna's teachings have been collected in several scriptures, including the Bhagavad Gita, the Mahabharata, and the Shrimad Bhagavatam.

Shri Krishna is not just a historical figure or a mythical character, but a beacon of hope and a major source of inspiration that touches the souls and hearts of people in ways that cannot be expressed in words.

Why are Shri Krishna's Teachings Important?

The teachings of Shri Krishna are most important because his teachings have a great power to transform you into a better human being and to transform your life at a deep spiritual level so that you can connect with your true self to find meaning and purpose in your life.

His teachings always remind us that we all are connected.

How are Shri Krishna's Teachings Useful?

The teachings of Shri Krishna offer timeless wisdom relevant to modern life. His teachings will not only help you towards the path of spiritual growth and enlightenment but also help you in achieving your career goals and success, in study and exam times, in love life and work life, on the path of self-development and personality development, goodness and compassion, in finding life purpose and happiness, in earning money and acquiring wealth, in making excellently adorned characters, in creating a royal lifestyle, and in achieving many more things.

Why Should You Read This Book?

You should read this book because Krishna's teachings are not just intellectual; they offer a road map for your entire life. His teachings will work like an expert guide when you find yourself struggling with the circumstances and challenges that life throws your way.

This book offers a practical and inspiring guide to living a happy life based on the teachings of Shri Krishna.

THE TEACHINGS OF SHRI KRISHNA

Teaching: 01

Do not Disrespect the Woman

"That incomparable radiance that was born from all Gods and Pervaded the three worlds, came to one place and took the form of a Woman."

— **Devimahatmyam-2.13**

The Shri Krishna avatar (incarnation) is one of the most colorful avatars, as are all Mahavishnu's avatars. As he is known to be the wisest teacher ever could be, whose song, The Bhagavad Gita, is the summary—the quintessence—of all the wisdom of our scriptures. He sometimes confuses us with the way he lived his entire life: "Whether he was a womanizer or a protector of women; whether he wanted to steal butter or our problems, and so on."

First, we should understand that we are not the body; we have a soul inside this material dress of the body. The body, the material dressed for the soul, changes from moment to moment as it develops and will constantly change until death. The body is subject to change, but the soul is not. In this world, males and females are the only gender designations assigned to different temporary body types, but spiritually, everyone is equal. We should change the bodily concept of life to think, "I am a man" or "I am a woman." It is an illusion.

But how can I claim that Krishna believed in women's empowerment? Especially, when we are constantly led to believe that he had romantic relationships with Gopikas and the Radha and that he had over 16,000 wives. It is believed that he had killed the rakshasi (Putna) in his childhood.

In accordance with the scripture Bhagavatam, the Gopikas were already sages in their previous lives. They made the choice to take birth as Gopikas in order to come closer to the sacred incarnation of Lord Vishnu.

Even after becoming King, Krishna maintained women's liberty in mind. It is commonly known that He married Rukmani only after she informed Sri Krishna that she did not wish to marry the groom picked by her brother. Rukmani had made up her mind to marry Sri Krishna. And Sri Krishna was happy to oblige. Similarly, when His sister Subadhra expressed her wish to marry Arjuna rather than Duryodhana (as Balabhadra had arranged), He pushed Arjuna and Subadhra to escape. In fact, He clearly instructed Arjuna to ensure that Subadhra rode the chariot. We wish we should have a Krishna in our midst when we hear about a young girl being loved by a young man. It is my view through the points written in the scriptures.

What about his 16,000 wives? Shri Krishna had rescued them from Jarasandha's Haram. It was the only way he could have provided them with a decent life free of ridicule and worries about their previous families' dependence.

Close your eyes and envision a world where every woman is treated with the respect, dignity, and honour she deserves. A world where her voice is heard, her dreams are valued, and her worth is recognized. Shri Krishna, the divine guide, urges us not to remain silent when a woman is disrespected. He reminds us of our responsibility to protect and uplift the women in our lives, fostering a culture of equality, compassion, and empowerment.

Krishna teaches us that women are not mere objects or possessions but sacred beings, embodying the divine feminine energy. He honoured and revered the women in his life—Radha, Draupadi, and countless others—recognizing their immense strength, wisdom, and contributions.

Draupadi, the woman blamed responsible for the Mahabharata war, is Sri Krishna's friend. She calls Him 'Sakha' - friend. Sri Krishna has often defended her honour, whether it was during the 'Vastra Haran' - disrobing in the open court - or when Sage Durvasa needed to be fed after the Pandavas and she had finished their meal. Even as they are discussing peace, He tells Draupadi that she would take her revenge on the Kauravas. He will never forget the humiliation heaped on her simply. He empowers women by telling them that they will be avenged and encourages them to never forget their shame.

There is no jewel like a woman. The man who loves his mother treats women wonderfully. A woman (mother) brought you into this world. We should not remain silent when a woman is disrespected. One of the most common verses among the sacred scriptures of Hinduism is: -

"Where Women are Honoured, Divinity Blossoms there and where they are Dishonoured, all actions remain unfruitful."

— **ManuSmriti-3.56**

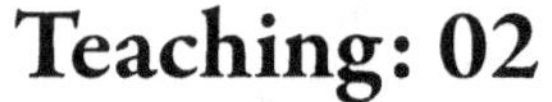

Teaching: 02

Sacrifice Comfort If You Aim for Success

"Success belongs to those who possess the courage to confront their fears and push beyond self-imposed limitations. Let bravery be your ally, and success shall bow to your indomitable spirit."

— Mahabharata

True success is beyond the sphere of comfort, and in order to achieve it, we must be willing to forego the convenience and assurance that comfort brings.

Close your eyes and imagine a life of ease, where every desire is satisfied, and every block is gone. It may appear attractive, but we know deep down that true progress and fulfilment lie beyond our comfort zones. Shri Krishna teaches us that success is the triumph over barriers through sacrifice and effort, not simply the absence of obstacles.

In the Bhagavad Gita, Krishna's teachings highlight the example of Arjuna, the renowned warrior. On the battlefield of Kurukshetra, Arjuna experienced severe inner turmoil. Overwhelmed by emotions, he considered leaving the war and taking refuge in his comfort zone.

Shri Krishna, on the other hand, encouraged him to recognize the importance of sacrificing his comfort for the greater good.

Lord Shri Krishna's life is proof of this philosophy. His life illustrates the bravery required to forego comfort in pursuit of greater aims.

He could have led a life of wealth and leisure because he was born into a Royal family. Nonetheless, he chose a path of selflessness and sacrifice, committing his life to helping humanity and preserving righteousness.

The Kurukshetra war, recounted in the epic Mahabharata, is one of the most notable examples of Krishna's willingness to forego comfort. Despite being a member of the royal family, Krishna did not hesitate to serve as a charioteer for his companion Arjuna, who was a skilled warrior. Krishna selflessly offered her services and his advice, despite the enormous hardships and sacrifices that were ahead.

As we consider Krishna's teachings, we must evaluate our own lives to see where we are clinging to comfort at the expense of advancement. Are we remaining in unsatisfying jobs because they provide security? Are we avoiding unpleasant conversations out of fear of being uncomfortable? Are we settling for less to make fewer sacrifices?

Shri Krishna, as a heavenly guide, pushes us to step outside of our comfort zones and face the challenges that life throws at us. He reminds us of those tackling obstacles head-on leads to growth.

Meanwhile, the sacrifices we make on our journey to success contribute to a greater sense of fulfilment and contentment. When we look back on our path, we realise that the obstacles we overcame and the comfort we gave up on helped shape us into better people.

It is critical to retain a sense of balance as we proceed on the path of sacrifice. Sacrificing our comfort does not suggest ignoring or surrendering our principles.

The route to success is constructed with the stones of sacrifice, and only those who tread upon them with unshakable determination shall find the treasures of triumph.

So, my dear friends, let us have the courage to sacrifice comfort for the sake of our aspirations. Let us step boldly into the unknown, guided by the wisdom of Shri Krishna. With each sacrifice we make, we inch closer to our true calling, creating a life of purpose, fulfilment, and extraordinary success. One of the most inspiring Quotations, which directly indicating towards showing determination, dedication, and sacrifice for achieving success is:

"Success comes to those who are disciplined, self-controlled, and dedicated to their pursuits. With righteous actions and a pure heart, one can overcome any obstacle and rise above mediocrity."

— ManuSmriti

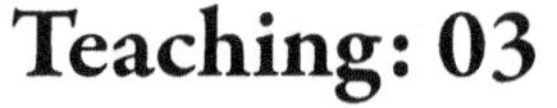

Teaching: 03

Treat Everyone Equally

"He who is equal-minded towards the good-hearted, friends, enemies, the indifferent, neutrals, haters, relations, towards the righteous and also the wicked, excels."
— Shrimad Bhagavad Gita-6.09

Krishna teaches us that every soul is born equal, regardless of their background, appearance, or social standing. He invites us to look beyond the external façade and recognize the eternal essence within each individual. Just as the sun's rays reach everyone equally, Krishna's love and compassion extend to all without discrimination. It is this love that he urges us to cultivate within ourselves. When we treat everyone equally, we become conduits of Krishna's divine love. We begin to see the interconnectedness of all beings, understanding that we are part of a vast cosmic tapestry where each thread is essential. In this tapestry, every colour, every texture, and every pattern contribute to the beauty and harmony of the whole.

Consider a world in which everyone is treated with kindness, respect, and equity. A world in which differences are celebrated and togetherness reigns supreme. Shri Krishna, the epitome of infinite love, shares this vision with us. Krishna reminds us that at the core of our being, we are not defined by our external appearances, social status, or material possessions.

Close your eyes for a moment and reflect on your own experiences. Have you ever felt excluded or judged based on your appearance, beliefs, or social status? How did it make you feel? Now, envision a different scenario where you are accepted and appreciated for who you are, and everyone is seen as a unique expression of divinity. This is the world that Shri Krishna envisions for us—one filled with love, compassion, and equality.

In the Bhagavad Gita, Krishna tells Arjuna that all beings are equal in the eyes of God. He says, "He who sees Me in all beings and all beings in Me, never loses Me, nor do I ever lose him." This teaching is based on the principle of Advaita, or non-duality. In Advaita, there is no separation between the individual soul and the Supreme Soul. We are all part of the same divine consciousness.

Krishna's teachings teach us that equality extends beyond the boundaries of race, religion, or gender. Just as a gardener nurtures every plant with equal care, we can cultivate a mindset of inclusivity and compassion towards all beings. It encompasses every being, whether human, animal, or nature itself. Treat the Earth with reverence, recognizing that our interconnectedness extends beyond human interactions. Let your choices reflect a deep sense of responsibility and respect for all forms of life. Recognize that no one is superior or inferior and that each person's contribution to the world is valuable.

Let us remember that treating everyone equally is an emotional commitment that comes from the depths of our souls, not just an academic exercise. It is a firm belief in the intrinsic value and dignity of every soul. When we internalize this concept, our actions reflect Krishna's teachings, and we become positive change agents in the world.

Krishna's message is simple: no one is unimportant, and everyone has an essential role to play in the magnificent tapestry of the world.

Let us carry the torch of equality and shed its light in every corner of our lives as we move through our own journey. By embracing Shri Krishna's teachings, we become change agents, transforming our families, communities, and the world at large. Each modest act of kindness, each gesture of inclusion, creates a ripple effect of love and equality.

So, my dear friends, let us make a commitment today—to treat everyone equally, to see the divinity within each person we encounter, and to spread the message of love and unity that Shri Krishna so passionately imparts. Together, we can create a world where equality is not just an aspiration but a living reality, a world where the timeless wisdom of Krishna guides us to live harmoniously as one human family.

"There is no distinction between high and low, rich, and poor, man and woman, or any other kind of difference. We are all equal in the eyes of God."

— Mahabharata

Teaching: 04

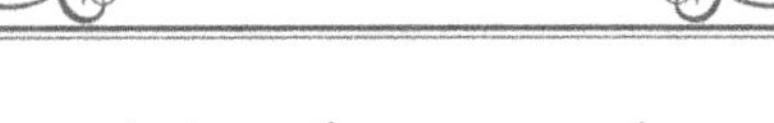

Everything Happens for A Reason

"Everything happens according to God's plan. Trust in Him, and He will guide you through the darkness."

— Valmiki Ramayana

Shri Krishna, the epitome of infinite wisdom, teaches us that everything happens for a reason—a profound lesson that can shift our perspective and bring us peace in the challenges that life brings.

As we deal with the ups and downs of life, it is critical to remember that Shri Krishna's teachings provide us with tremendous insight into the intricate workings of the cosmos. Through the concept of "everything happens for a reason," Krishna presses us to investigate the deeper meaning behind each incident, recognizing that there is a divine plan unfolding that is beyond our present comprehension.

Krishna encourages us to accept the idea that life is a sequence of interconnected occurrences that are delicately woven together for our growth and development.

Every happy experience and every terrible scenario help to shape us into the people we are destined to be. Our spiritual growth and change are influenced by the lessons we learn, the relationships we make, and the challenges we experience.

When confronted with adversity or unexpected outcomes, it is natural to wonder why certain things happen. On the other hand, Krishna reminds us that our perspective is limited, and what appears to be a setback or a difficulty in the present moment may be a stepping stone toward a bigger goal. We can find solace and calm by growing trust in the divine plan and understanding that every circumstance is an opportunity for us to learn, evolve, and accomplish our supreme purpose.

The phrase "everything happens for a reason" reminds us that we are a part of something bigger than ourselves. Finally, the deep concept that everything happens for a reason holds the potential to change our perspective on life's obstacles.

"Even the most difficult times can be turned into opportunities for growth and learning."

— Ramayana

Teaching: 05

Always Keeps Smiling

"Always keep a cheerful face and speak words that are sweet and pleasing."

— Lord Krishna

A common interpretation of Krishna's smile is that it represents his joy, happiness, and love for all living things. According to stories, his grin has the potential to calm even the most disturbed mind and warm the iciest heart.

Shri Krishna, the divine incarnate, teaches us how to live a happy and fulfilled life. He motivates us to stay positive and smile no matter what life throws at us. In this short lesson, we will look at Shri Krishna's wisdom and discover how to maintain a smile even in inconvenient situations.

Shri Krishna's teachings highlight the necessity of keeping a joyful and optimistic attitude. He reminds us that the world is full of ups and downs, but our attitude dictates how we see them. We may nurture an optimistic mindset, attract positive energy, and generate joy and happiness in our lives by keeping a smile on our faces.

Smiling is more than just a happy expression; it also has a significant impact on our physical and mental well-being. According to research, smiling releases endorphins, which are natural painkillers that can boost emotions of pleasure and contentment. Smiling can also help to reduce stress, regulate blood pressure, and strengthen the immune system. We can improve our general health and well-being by maintaining a positive attitude.

Life is full of obstacles, and we occasionally find ourselves in situations that are overwhelming and disappointing. Shri Krishna's wisdom advises us to keep smiling and maintain a pleasant attitude in such conditions. We can overcome problems with grace and resilience, discovering creative solutions and possibilities for growth.

Shri Krishna's teachings also emphasize the value of a compassionate smile. When we smile with kindness and warmth, we elevate the moods of those around us, causing a positive and benevolent ripple effect. A smile can brighten someone's day, relieve their load, and form a bond of love and understanding.

Smiling, like any other habit, can be fostered and nurtured. We can train ourselves to smile more often, even when things are not going well. We may adjust our thinking and create an enjoyable experience for ourselves and those around us by smiling intentionally.

Furthermore, Krishna's smile serves as a reminder of the power of resilience and strength in the face of hardship. Life throws many challenges our way, but when we face them with a smile, we show an unshakeable desire to overcome obstacles. A grin represents our inner strength and steadfast faith in the Almighty.

Let us then embrace Krishna's instructions and infuse our lives with their light. Let us choose to wear a smile that reflects our inner light and invites happiness, love, and perseverance through the ups and downs.

❖ A smile is a lethal weapon. Even the most antagonistic person can be disarmed by it.

❖ A smile denotes satisfaction. When you smile, you are telling the world that you are happy and content.

❖ A smile spreads like wildfire. When you smile at someone, they are more likely to return your smile. This action can set off a positive energy chain reaction.

❖ A smile is an expression of communication. It expresses a wide range of emotions, including happiness and love.

So, while you go about your day, remember the transforming power that exists inside you. Krishna's smile is more than just a physical expression; it reflects his state of consciousness. Keep smiling since it holds the secret to a life filled with love, serenity, joy, and boundless happiness.

In my conclusion, Shri Krishna's teachings serve as a reminder of the healing power of a smile. We may develop a positive outlook, enhance our physical and mental health, overcome obstacles with grace and resiliency, spread kindness and compassion, and start a positive chain reaction in the world by maintaining a positive attitude. Let us emulate Shri Krishna's example and never stop grinning, bringing joy and happiness with us everywhere we go.

"The face is the mirror of the soul. A smiling face shows a happy soul."

— Unknown

Teaching: 06

Importance Of Karma

"**What is action and what is inaction? Even the wise are confused in determining this. Now I shall explain to you the secret of action, by knowing which, you may free yourself from material bondage.**"

— Bhagavad Gita-4.16

Karma is a Sanskrit word that means "action". or "deed." Every action we perform is like a brushstroke on the canvas of our destiny in the divine tapestry of life. Shri Krishna, the incarnation of compassion and wisdom, reveals the profound meaning of karma and its transformative power in our lives. As we dwell on the concept, we realise that every thought, word, and deed have a ripple effect that shapes our present and future.

For a moment, close your eyes and envision a world in which every action you take has no impact, no rippling effect. Consider a world in which your decisions and actions are meaningless. Imagine a reality where we are not accountable for the seeds we sow. It is a bleak and chaotic vision devoid of purpose and growth. It is a depressing and meaningless world.

Krishna's teachings are beautiful because they are applicable. He reminds us that we do not have to be overwhelmed by the gravity of our deeds or the complexities of life. Instead, Krishna advises us to focus on the present moment and fulfil our jobs sincerely. Every role, whether parent, teacher, student, or professional, provides an arena for karmic unfoldment.

Karma can be classified into two categories: Good Karma and Bad Karma. Positive behaviours such as kindness, compassion, and being helpful create good karma. Negative behaviours such as cruelty, selfishness, or injury create bad karma.

We will reap what we sow, according to the rules of karma. This indicates that good karma creates positive experiences in our future lives, whereas bad karma creates terrible events.

Karma is not a law of punishment or reward. Everything comes down to cause and effect. Our actions have effects, both now and in the future.

Krishna's karma teachings serve as a gentle reminder that we are not merely bystanders in life's magnificent performance. We are actively shaping our future as co-creators. No matter how minor or small our acts may seem, they all play a part in the complex web of existence. Our actions can effect change, healing, and growth, much like the soft wind that rustles the leaves or the raindrop that saturates the parched land.

Here are some examples of how karma can manifest in our lives:

❖ If we are kind to others, they are more likely to be kind to us.

❖ If we are helpful to others, they are more likely to help us.

❖ If we are honest, others are more likely to trust us.

THE TEACHINGS OF SHRI KRISHNA

❖ If we are hardworking, we are more likely to be successful.

❖ If we are grateful, we are more likely to attract good things into our lives.

On the other hand, if we are cruel to others, they are more likely to be hostile towards us. If we are selfish, others are more likely to be selfish towards us. If we are dishonest, others are more likely to lie to us. If we are lazy, we are less likely to be successful. If we are ungrateful, we are more likely to attract bad things into our lives.

Close your eyes for a moment and picture a world where every deed, thought, and purpose is noted. Where each action you performed—every step you took, every word you spoke, every gesture you made—could determine your future and affect the lives of others. This is the fundamental idea of Krishna's karma teachings—that our deeds have repercussions, both in this life and the next.

Think of karma as the seeds we sow in the fertile soil of our lives. If we sow seeds of kindness, love, and compassion, we will reap a bountiful harvest of joy, fulfilment, and harmonious relationships. Conversely, if we sow seeds of negativity, selfishness, and harm, we will inevitably reap the bitter fruits of suffering and discord.

The law of karma helps us understand why good people sometimes face terrible things. If we believe that everyone is responsible for their karma, then we can see that terrible things may happen not as punishment but because of negative actions in a previous life.

Krishna's wisdom on karma is a treasure trove of life lessons. He teaches us that it is not just about the results; it is about the purity of our intentions and the selflessness in our actions. When we let go of our selfish desires, something extraordinary happens. We connect with a higher power and rise above our ego's demands. Krishna reveals an incredible truth: we have the power to shape our destiny. By setting our intentions wisely and acting selflessly, we can transform our lives and create a ripple of positivity that spreads everywhere. So, let us embrace Krishna's timeless teachings and unlock the incredible power of karma. Get ready for a journey of personal growth and the realization of your true potential. It is time to make magic happen! Shape your destiny, spread positivity, and create a meaningful world.

"Those who see action in inaction and inaction in action are truly wise amongst humans. Although performing all kinds of actions, they are yogis and masters of all their actions."

— Bhagavad Gita-4.18

Teaching: 07

Live In the Present

"The past is already gone, the future is uncertain, but the present moment is within our control. By fully dedicating ourselves to the present, we can experience the eternal bliss of the divine presence."

— Shrimad Bhagavatam

Living in the present moment is valuable for navigating life's complexities. The Bhagavad Gita offers timeless wisdom on embracing the present fully. By embodying these teachings, we connect more deeply with ourselves, others, and the divine. This chapter explores Gita's teachings, emphasizing the significance of living in the present and offering practical insights to do so.

The Bhagavad Gita says the present moment is where our true power lies. We should focus on it and use our energy wisely. Krishna's teachings help us see the potential in the present moment and use it for personal growth and change.

Dwelling on the past holds us back and stops us from fully engaging in the present. Krishna advises us to let go of regrets, grudges, and longing for what is gone. By freeing from the past, we open our hearts to the present possibilities. Let us go and create a brighter future.

The Bhagavad Gita says: Do not obsess over the future. It is good to plan and prepare, but Krishna tells us to let go of worries and desires for specific results. Trust in the divine plan and embrace uncertainty. Focus on the present, find peace, and build resilience.

Mindfulness helps us live in the present. Bhagavad Gita emphasizes it too. Krishna advises being fully present in actions, thoughts, and emotions. By practicing mindfulness, we can observe our experiences without judgement, heightening our awareness and deepening our connection to the present moment. It allows us to be fully engaged with life's wonders. Let us cherish each moment, finding beauty in small things.

The Bhagavad Gita teaches that true joy or contentment is found in the present moment. Fully immersing ourselves in what we do leads to fulfillment and happiness. Krishna advises us to enjoy simple pleasures, appreciate beauty, and be grateful for our blessings.

Living in the present moment transforms our lives positively. It brings intention, joy, and spiritual awareness. The Bhagavad Gita teaches us to embrace the power of the now, let go of past attachments and future worries, and cultivate mindfulness and gratitude. By integrating these teachings, we connect deeply with ourselves, others, and the divine. This leads to a fulfilling and purposeful existence. Let us follow Krishna's wisdom and embark on the journey of living fully in the present.

"The wise person does not grieve for the past or worry about the future. The wise person lives in the present moment and is content with what they have."

Teaching: 08

Think With a Calm Mind

"Calmness, gentleness, silence, self-restraint, and purity: these are the disciplines of the mind."

—Lord Krishna

This chapter "Think with a Calm Mind," where we explore the teachings of Lord Krishna and how they emphasize the importance of maintaining a composed and clear mind in various situations. Throughout this chapter, we will journey through stories and lessons from Krishna's life, uncovering the wisdom behind his serene demeanor and wise counsel. From his childhood antics to his role as a teacher on the battlefield of Kurukshetra, we will discover how Krishna's tranquil mind guided him through challenges and offered profound insights for us to learn from.

Let us start with Krishna's childhood, where his playful antics often held profound lessons. Once, when Krishna was caught eating mud by his mother Yashoda, she scolded him and asked him to open his mouth. Instead of mud, she saw the entire universe within Krishna's mouth. This incident amazed Yashoda and made her realize the divine nature of her son. It teaches us that even in playful moments, Krishna maintained a calm and composed demeanor, revealing the vastness of existence.

Moving on to Krishna's youth, we encounter his role as a fearless warrior. Despite facing numerous challenges and threats from demons sent by his evil uncle Kamsa, Krishna remained composed and resolute. He not only defended himself but also protected his loved ones and the people of Vrindavan from harm. Through his courage and calmness in the face of danger, Krishna exemplified the power of a tranquil mind to overcome adversity.

As Krishna matured into a king, he faced various political and diplomatic challenges. However, he approached each situation with equanimity and wisdom, always acting in accordance with dharma (righteousness). Krishna's mastery of strategy and leadership skills allowed him to navigate complex situations with grace and clarity of mind. His example teaches us the importance of maintaining composure and making decisions thoughtfully, even in times of uncertainty.

Finally, we come to Krishna's role as a teacher, particularly during the great battle of Kurukshetra. Here, he imparted profound teachings to his disciple Arjuna, guiding him through moments of doubt and confusion. Krishna's teachings on yoga, bhakti, and Vedanta emphasized the importance of maintaining a calm mind and performing one's duty without attachment to the results. Through his guidance, Arjuna found clarity and resolve, ready to face his challenges with renewed strength.

The life and teachings of Lord Krishna offer invaluable lessons on the importance of thinking with a calm mind. From his childhood to his role as a teacher and guide, Krishna demonstrated the transformative power of maintaining composure and clarity in all aspects of life. As we reflect on his example, may we cultivate a tranquil mind, capable of navigating life's challenges with wisdom and grace.

"For one who has conquered his mind, a mind is best of friends, but for one who has failed to do so, a mind is the greatest enemy."

—Lord Krishna

About The Author

Sachin Prajapati is an AI enthusiast, seeker of wisdom, and passionate writer. His journey spans the realms of code, consciousness, and cosmic contemplation. With a background in Computer Science & Engineering and a specialization in Artificial Intelligence and Machine Learning, Sachin merges technical expertise with spiritual curiosity.

Growing up in the culturally rich land of India, Sachin was drawn to ancient texts and timeless teachings. His fascination with the Bhagavad Gita, the Mahabharata, and the sacred scriptures led him on a profound quest for understanding. Through extensive study, meditation, and contemplation, he gained insights into the profound wisdom encapsulated in Krishna's words.

In "The Teachings of Shri Krishna," Sachin weaves together ancient wisdom and contemporary understanding. His commitment to bridging the gap between sacred texts and modern thought makes this book a valuable resource for seekers of all backgrounds. Whether exploring neural networks or unraveling cosmic mysteries, Sachin's writing reflects a deep reverence for both science and spirituality.

Beyond the binary code, Sachin finds solace in the music of the flute and the serenity of yoga. His cup of chai is not just a beverage; it is a moment of reflection. For him, knowledge resides not only in data points but also in the depths of the heart.

THE TEACHINGS OF SHRI KRISHNA

In Sachin's universe, enlightenment is not a destination—it is a recursive function.

Points To Remember from Chapters

Chapter: 1

- ❖ Krishna, an avatar of Lord Vishnu, embodies wisdom and compassion, as demonstrated in the Bhagavad Gita.
- ❖ Despite historical narratives, Krishna's relationships with women, like Radha and Draupadi, were based on respect and empowerment.
- ❖ Krishna respected women's autonomy, supporting Rukmani and Subadhra in their marital choices.
- ❖ He rescued 16,000 wives to provide them with dignity and security, showing his commitment to women's well-being.
- ❖ Krishna's teachings emphasize the importance of honoring and empowering women, fostering a culture of equality and compassion.

Chapter: 2

- ❖ Success requires facing fears and surpassing self-imposed limits.

- In the Bhagavad Gita, Krishna advises Arjuna to sacrifice comfort for the greater good.
- Despite being born into royalty, Krishna chose selflessness and served as Arjuna's charioteer in the Kurukshetra war.
- Sacrificing comfort leads to personal growth and fulfillment on the path to success.
- Sacrificing comfort doesn't mean compromising values; it's about facing challenges with determination and guidance from Shri Krishna.

Chapter: 3

- Krishna's Teaching: Krishna says we should treat everyone the same, no matter how they look or where they're from.
- Imagine a Fair World: Picture a world where everyone is treated kindly and with respect, regardless of their differences.
- From the Bhagavad Gita: In a book called the Bhagavad Gita, Krishna tells us that we're all equal in the eyes of God.
- Equality in Action: Treating everyone fairly includes not just people, but also animals and nature.
- Promise to Treat Everyone Fairly: Let's commit to treating everyone equally, spreading love and unity just like Krishna wants us to.

Chapter: 4

- ❖ Shri Krishna teaches that everything happens for a reason, meaning there's a plan behind everything.
- ❖ Life's ups and downs help us grow and become who we're meant to be.
- ❖ Even when things seem tough, there's a bigger picture we might not see yet.
- ❖ Trusting in this bigger plan can give us comfort and help us stay calm in hard times.
- ❖ Every experience, good or bad, teaches us something valuable and helps us grow.

Chapter: 5

- ❖ Shri Krishna teaches us to always smile, spreading joy and warmth to others.
- ❖ Keeping a cheerful attitude, even in tough times, can make a big difference in how we feel.
- ❖ Smiling has many health benefits, like reducing stress and boosting our mood.
- ❖ By smiling, we can also uplift others and create a positive atmosphere around us.
- ❖ Let's remember Krishna's wisdom and keep smiling, bringing happiness wherever we go.

Chapter: 6

- Karma means our actions and deeds, shaping our present and future.
- Every action we take has consequences, whether positive or negative.
- Good karma brings positive experiences, while bad karma leads to negative outcomes.
- Karma is not about punishment or reward; it's about cause and effect.
- By understanding karma, we can shape our destiny and create a more meaningful life.

Chapter: 7

- Focus on the present moment, as it holds our true power and potential.
- Let go of past regrets and future worries to fully engage with the present.
- Practice mindfulness to observe experiences without judgment and deepen connection to the present.
- Find joy and contentment in simple pleasures and appreciate the beauty of each moment.
- Living in the present transforms our lives positively, leading to fulfillment and spiritual awareness.

Chapter: 8

- Krishna's childhood antics, like eating mud, revealed profound lessons about maintaining composure even in playful moments.
- As a youth, Krishna faced threats from demons but remained composed and courageous, protecting his loved ones and his people.
- As a king, Krishna navigated political challenges with equanimity and wisdom, always acting in accordance with righteousness.
- During the battle of Kurukshetra, Krishna guided Arjuna through moments of doubt, emphasizing the importance of maintaining a calm mind and performing one's duty without attachment to results.
- Krishna's life teaches us the transformative power of thinking with a calm mind, enabling us to navigate life's challenges with wisdom and grace.

CHAPTER ONE

Blast Off

Normally the invasive blast of the alarm at 4:00 AM was an unwelcome intrusion, but not today. Jay immediately slapped the button to kill the noise, then instinctively rolled over, put a hand on Shanna's cheek, and kissed her forehead before bounding from bed. Jay was as excited as a small child on Christmas morning about today's fishing trip with his two brothers-in-law. Thankfully Shanna was an extremely sound sleeper, difficult to awaken in the early morning hours.

* * * * * * * * * * * * * * * * * * *

<u>**CHAPTER TWO**</u>

Preparation

The previous evening Daniel and James gathered at Jay's house, along with their wives, kids, and pets filling the comfortable abode with happy, yelling, laughing, chatting relatives. Excited kids, ran back and forth, in and out, carried cats, dragged dogs and the baby, while enjoying the bedlam and having a great time together.

During dinner, the sisters discussed their plans for the following day. It would be filled with shopping at the mall, trying out new winter clothes for the kids, finding sales on outfits they just couldn't live without, and finally a rare movie with